No Lex 10-12

RACE CAR LEGENDS

The Allisons

Mario Andretti

Dale Earnhardt

A. J. Foyt

Richard Petty

The Unsers

CHELSEA HOUSE PUBLISHERS

RICHARD PETTY

Ron Frankl

CHELSEA HOUSE PUBLISHERS
New York   Philadelphia

Produced by Daniel Bial and Associates
New York, New York

Picture research by Alan Gottlieb
Cover illustration by Robert Tannenbaum

First Printing

1 3 5 7 9 8 6 4 2

Library of Congress Cataloging-in-Publication Data

Frankl, Ron.
      Richard Petty / Ron Frankl.
         p.   cm. — (Race car legends)
      Includes bibliographical references and index.
      Summary: A biography which focuses in the racing career of
professional driver Richard Petty.
       ISBN 0-7910-3182-9 (hc). — ISBN 0-7910-3183-7 (pbk.)
       1. Petty, Richard—Juvenile literature.   2. Automobile racing drivers—
United States—Biography—Juvenile literature.   3. Daytona International
Speedway Race—Juvenile literature.
    [1. Petty, Richard   2. Automobile racing drivers.]
    I. Title.   II. Series
    GV1032.P47F73   1996
    796.7′2′092—dc20
    [B]   95-18216
                                            CIP
                                            AC

CONTENTS

THE DRIVE TO WIN

What's the most popular spectator sport in the United States? It's not baseball, football, basketball, or even horse racing. America's favorite sport is automobile racing.

To the outsider, it looks simple. You get in your car, keep the accelerator depressed as you hurtle around the track, expect your crew to keep the car in perfect condition, and try not to go deaf as you weave your machine through traffic toward the checkered flag. But in actuality, it's not at all easy. Just as baseball isn't simply a matter of hitting the ball, so racing is full of subtleties.

What does it take to be a world-class race car driver? The more you know about the lives of the greats, the more it becomes clear that each successful driver is an extraordinary athlete gifted with unusual vision, coordination, and the will to win. The concentration necessary to send a car speeding around a track at 200 miles per hour for hour after hour, when a momentary lapse can cause instant death for him and any unfortunate driver near him, is phenomenal. Any driver worth his salt must be strong, self-confident, resilient, and willing to take risks in order to have an opportunity to win.

In addition, the top drivers have to be good businessmen and know how to put together a winning team. They have to find sponsors to put them in competitive cars. They rely on a pit crew to make sure that their car is always in peak performance condition. And they have to be mentally prepared each race day to take into consideration a host of factors: weather, the other racers, the condition of the track, and how their car is responding on that day. Without everything right, a driver won't stand a chance of winning.

All the drivers in the Race Car Legends series grew up around race cars. The fathers of Richard Petty and Dale Earnhardt were very successful race car drivers themselves. A. J. Foyt's father was a part-time racer and a full-time mechanic; the Allisons and Unsers are an extended family of racers. Only Mario Andretti's father disapproved of his son's racing. Yet Mario and his twin brother Aldo devoted themselves to racing at a young age.

Despite the knowledge and connections a family can provide, few of the legendary racers portrayed in this series met with immediate success. They needed to prove themselves in sprint cars or midget cars before they were allowed to get behind the wheel of a contending stock car or a phenomenally expensive Indy car. They needed to be tested in the tough races on the hardscrabble tracks before they learned enough to handle the race situations at Daytona or the Brickyard. They needed to learn how to get the most out of whatever vehicle they were piloting, including knowing how to fix an engine in the wee hours of the night before a big race.

A driver also has to learn to face adversity, because crashes often take the lives of friends or relatives. Indeed, every driver has been lucky at one point or another to survive a scare or a bad accident. "We've had our tragedies, but what family hasn't?" remarked the mother of Al and Bobby Unser. "I don't blame racing. I love racing as our whole family has."

What each driver has proved is that success in this most grueling sport takes commitment. Walter Payton, the great football running back, and Paul Newman, star of many blockbuster movies, have both taken up racing—and proved they have some talent behind the wheel. Still, it's evident that neither has been able to provide the devotion it takes to be successful at the highest levels.

To be a great driver, racing has to be in your blood.

THE FINISH

Richard Petty won 200 races, almost twice as many victories as any other driver in the history of stock-car racing. His most famous finish, though, was a race he did not win.

It was February 15, 1976, and the event was the Daytona 500, the first race of the season. Daytona is as important to stock-car racing as the Super Bowl is to football or the World Series is to baseball. Unlike these and all other sports, though, stock-car racing begins its year with its biggest and most glamorous event.

The Daytona International Speedway 500 has a track 2½ miles long with a long straightaway and steeply banked turns that enable the cars to reach speeds of over 180 miles per hour. Although other races are held at the speedway, the Daytona 500 is always one of the most exciting and eagerly awaited races of the year.

The 1976 race did not disappoint the crowd, estimated at nearly 150,000. The millions of fans

The finish of the 1976 Daytona 500 was one of the most exciting in history.

9

who watched the race on television also got more than their money's worth. The most successful driver in the sport also had the most fans, and they were eager to see Richard Petty compete at a race he has won more often than anyone else. Petty had finished the 1975 season by winning his fourth driving championship in five years. This race marked Petty's 19th season of racing for the National Association of Stock Car Auto Racing (NASCAR), the organization that runs stock-car racing.

For most of the race, the 38-year-old Petty kept near the front of the pack. With 188 laps completed, Petty had his famous number 43 Plymouth only seconds behind David Pearson. Pearson, at age 41, was already a grandfather. A two-time national champion, he had been Petty's top rival for years. Now, with 12 laps to go, the man nicknamed "King Richard" had his car running faster than Pearson's. He swooped to the inside of the track and grabbed the lead.

Pearson stayed close behind Petty, though, and the two drivers roared toward the finish line. They had clearly established that their two cars were the fastest on the track, and all other drivers were left far behind them. The crowd was in a frenzy as they watched the two great competitors battle it out.

Petty, who had already won five times at the Daytona 500, could not pull away from Pearson. As the two cars entered the 200th and final lap, his lead was only a few feet. Suddenly, Pearson saw an opportunity, ducking his Mercury down toward the inside of the track. Using his car's momentum to "slingshot" past Petty, Pearson took a short lead.

With less than half a lap before they reached the finish line, Petty knew that he had only one chance remaining. As the two cars entered the fourth and final turn, Petty made his move, dipping down low in the turn and poking the nose of his car in front. It was beginning to look like another Daytona triumph for Petty.

Unfortunately, for one of the few times in his career, Petty miscalculated. As he moved ahead of Pearson, traveling at over 180 miles per hour, Petty attempted to slide his car outward, directly in front of Pearson. This way, he could block any attempt by his rival to regain the lead. Petty thought he had moved completely past Pearson, but he had not. The back of Petty's car hit the front of Pearson's. The contact caused both cars to skid out of control.

The tires of both cars gave off huge clouds of smoke as both Petty and Pearson struggled to regain command of their racing machines. The nose of Pearson's car made hard contact with the track wall, then he skidded across the track and onto the grass infield.

Meanwhile, it seemed for a moment that Petty might emerge with no serious damage. He had wrestled with the steering wheel and gotten the car straightened out when suddenly the front skidded up the track and into the wall with tremendous force. The collision with the wall badly damaged Petty's car, with most of the destruction occurring near the engine.

Petty's car began to spin around and around. Both the front and back slammed into the outer wall several times. Then he skidded down the track to the infield grass, where he finally came to a stop about 100 years short of the finish line.

David Pearson (left) was able to get his car to limp to the finish line. Petty was unable to restart his car and had to have it pushed.

Neither driver was seriously injured, but both cars looked like wrecks. Petty's engine was ruined, and though he tried repeatedly, he could not restart his car.

Pearson's car, however, still ran. Petty could do nothing but look on helplessly as Pearson inched his crippled car at a less-than-awesome speed of 20 miles per hour to take the checkered flag. It was Pearson's first Daytona victory.

No one who viewed this spectacular finish had ever seen anything like it. No stock-car race, at Daytona or elsewhere, had ever ended in such a dramatic fashion.

After the race, Petty accepted responsibility for causing the accident. He apologized to Pearson. Pearson accepted, and both men acknowledged it was all just part of racing.

What were Petty's emotions after the race? Naturally, he was disappointed to have lost. He was also grateful that no one was injured. But more than anything else, he had found the race thrilling. It was just as exciting for him to be in a great competition as it was for the spectators to watch it.

This was what the sport was all about.

2
STARTING OUT

Richard Petty was born on July 2, 1937, in Level Cross, a small town in North Carolina. The Petty family was poor, but no poorer than most of their neighbors. Like many of his schoolmates, Richard spent his early years in a house without electricity, running water, or a telephone.

Racing was a big part of Richard Petty's life from an early age. His father, Lee, was a champion stock-car racer who won 54 NASCAR races during his career. Lee began racing in 1947 at the unusually advanced age of 35. Before he turned to racing, Lee Petty supported his family by driving a delivery truck.

When NASCAR began to schedule races in June 1949, Lee Petty quit his job and began racing full-time. Although a kind and generous man off the track, Lee was one of the fiercest competitors in racing. His aggressive driving style

In the early days, Lee Petty—and all drivers—didn't bring their cars to the race sight on a flatbed. They drove them from track to track.

enabled him to win three driving championships. He was one of the most popular drivers with stock-car racing fans as NASCAR began to grow and prosper.

Formed by a group of drivers, race promoters, and car owners, NASCAR was formed in 1948 to ensure an honest and exciting standard of racing. Rules to ensure honest competition were made, and prize money for the drivers was guaranteed. The idea for NASCAR came from William France, a promoter and former driver, who saw the potential for stock-car racing to become a major spectator sport. Although NASCAR was run like a private club, the organization was a private company that was owned and controlled by France and his family.

In 1949, NASCAR's first season of racing, no superspeedways had yet been built, and most races were held at small speedways with unpaved dirt tracks. At Daytona, Florida, they raced on a course that was actually set up on the beach. Most drivers built and owned their cars, with no sponsors to help them pay their expenses. The prize money was small; no one grew wealthy from stock-car racing. Instead, the drivers raced simply because they loved racing.

In 1952, races in Daytona, Florida, took place on the sandy beaches.

Lee Petty built and tested his race cars at a machine shop and small test track right on the Petty property. Nearby, Richard, his younger brother, Maurice, and cousin Dale Inman pursued their own type of racing, staging bicycle races on a course they made for their regular use. Despite fierce competition from his playmates, Richard usually won. The Petty family was close, and Richard had a stable and happy childhood.

Lee Petty's little machine shop would one day grow into Petty Enterprises, a thriving business with several dozen employees devoted to building race cars. During Richard's childhood, though, the shop was nothing more than a converted tool shed with a dirt floor. There were no employees. Lee Petty did all the work himself, at least until Richard and Maurice were old enough to help. Before they were in high school, the boys were spending their weekends and after-school hours working with their father on his race cars. The whole family, including the boys' mother, Elizabeth, would often go to the speedways and share a picnic lunch before the race.

Richard and Maurice both became excellent mechanics. They eagerly assisted their father in perfecting the cars that helped him become the most successful driver on the Grand National schedule, NASCAR's highest level.

In addition to their garage work at Petty Enterprises, the boys accompanied their father to his races on the weekends. With their cousin Dale they served as his pit crew, changing tires, filling the gasoline tank, and making minor repairs during each race. Richard Petty quickly grew to love the racing world, and knew that he wanted a career in the sport. Surprisingly, though, when he was a teenager, Richard had no interest in being a driver. Instead, both he and Maurice wanted to become mechanics.

The term *stock car* suggests that the automobiles are exactly the same as those available to the public, a car taken directly from the car maker's stock. When NASCAR started, it was intended that the cars be based on models currently available from the major automobile manufacturers. Parts from other types of cars, or specially made by the driver, were against the rules. The mechanics could make only minor modifications and adjustments, although many tried to bend the rules by secretly using parts that were illegal under NASCAR rules. Drivers who were found to have cheated were fined or suspended.

Over the years, the restrictions regarding the use of "non-stock" parts were gradually relaxed. Today, stock cars are as different as can be from normal passenger sedans. Although the body of the car and engine are adapted from a recent model, the suspension, steering, brakes, and other elements of the car are specially made for racing. The only rule is that the parts used must be available to the public.

Although NASCAR has very specific rules covering such areas as the car's parts, weight, and engine size, car builders have much freedom as to how they build and adjust their racers. As a result, there is a big difference in performance from one car to the next. A talented mechanic tries not only to increase the car's speed but also to assemble a car that handles well, gets efficient gas mileage, and can run dependably throughout a long race. Building and testing cars is time-consuming and tedious

Richard Petty drives his father's car (number 42) in a 1958 convertible race at Darlington, South Carolina.

work, but it is essential for success on the track.

Lee Petty was one of the best car builders in the early years of NASCAR, and his efforts in the garage led to success on the track. He also taught his sons well, and the Pettys soon developed a reputation in NASCAR for building the best race cars.

Richard Petty attended nearby Randleman High School. Tall and athletic, he played baseball, basketball, and football, and he seemed to excel at every sport. After graduating in 1955, he went to work full-time for Petty Enterprises.

While he enjoyed working and contributing to his father's tremendous success, Richard soon realized he wanted something more in his life. He missed the excitement and competition he had experienced in high school sports.

Richard was testing a car on the Petty Enterprises test track when it occurred to him that he, too, wanted to try racing. Lee Petty was not eager to see his sons follow him into racing careers. Maurice was happy to develop his skills as a master mechanic, but Richard was determined to drive.

Lee told Richard that if he wished to pursue a career as a driver, he would have to wait until he reached his 21st birthday. The elder Petty hoped that the wait would cause Richard to change his mind and stick to the garage. Reluctantly, Richard agreed to wait, knowing that without his father's assistance he could not afford to race on his own. He spent the next three years patiently working behind the scenes at Petty Enterprises, never once asking his father for the opportunity to get behind the wheel.

Finally, shortly after he turned 21 in July 1958, Richard approached his father again and asked him to let him drive. On a night when Lee was scheduled to race in Asheville, North Carolina, a convertible class race was scheduled in Columbia, South Carolina. (NASCAR had a schedule of races for open-roofed, "convertible," cars at the time.) Richard wanted to enter the Asheville race, and asked his father, "Can I try?"

This time, Lee relented. "Yeah, okay, there's a car. Go get it, fix it up, and take it to the race."

With one of his father's old cars, a 1957 Oldsmobile, and his cousin Dale to head his pit crew, Richard Petty headed to Columbia for his first race. He was almost completely inexperienced, having never driven in any kind of formal race. Petty would be making his racing debut at a major track, competing against drivers who were older and far more competition-savvy. His greatest worry before the race, though, was whether he would have the endurance to survive 200 hard-fought laps around the track.

"I was not trying to win that first race," Petty recalled years later. "I just wanted to finish and I was looking for a driving style that would be comfortable for me."

Petty ran the 13th-fastest qualifying lap before the race, and therefore the rookie driver started the race in the 13th position from the front. As the green flag was waved and the race began, an excited Petty was surprised at how much he was enjoying the race.

"That was the first time I ever got in a race car and went tearing down in to the corner to see how hard I could go," Petty remembered later. "I felt comfortable with it."

Petty ran a good race. Although he took few chances and was concentrating mostly on avoiding serious tangles with the other drivers, he was able to weave his way through traffic and pass many slower cars. When the checkered flag came down, Petty was in sixth place, six laps behind the winner.

It was a very impressive debut. Petty had demonstrated the ability necessary to race and, more importantly, he had started to find himself.

More than ever before, Richard Petty was convinced that his future was in the driver's seat.

3

LEARNING THE GAME

Richard Petty was committed to a racing career after his surprising sixth place finish in his first race. He had demonstrated potential as a racer, but natural ability alone does not make a good driver. Qualities such as sharp reflexes, physical strength, and tremendous courage are vital in becoming a productive driver. They do not, however, guarantee success.

A winning driver also needs good judgment and racing knowledge, both of which can only develop from experience on the track. Even the greatest racers must go through a long and often painful learning process before they perform well on a regular basis.

Richard Petty struggled on the racetrack after his promising debut. "I was so cocky from that first race that I think I wrecked in my next three races," Petty recalled years later. He displayed good racing instincts, but he also made many

Richard Petty learned to be a great driver by being a great mechanic first.

mistakes. Spinouts and accidents happened frequently throughout the rest of his races during 1958, his rookie NASCAR season. Despite these difficulties, it was obvious that Petty was learning quickly and was improving as a driver with every race.

"I learned to drive by driving," Petty commented in retrospect. "There is no school where someone can teach you on the blackboard. You have to get in that car and hit the walls and find out all about it for yourself."

Petty's confidence grew with every race. He began his career on the Grand National circuit, NASCAR's top level, so he learned how to race while competing against the best drivers in the business. Few other racers have had this opportunity.

Despite the number of cars Richard wrecked in his first season, Lee Petty did not regret the addition of his son as the junior driver for Petty Enterprises. The elder Petty was at the peak of his career, and he could afford to help his son at the beginning of his new career. It was a good situation for Richard, too, because his father's support allowed him to concentrate on improving his skills as a driver. Many young drivers must struggle to find a regular driving job, and often the cars that they pilot are not competitive with the fastest machines on the track.

Built and serviced by Petty Enterprises, Petty's car was good enough to run with the leaders in each race. As his driving ability grew and the frequency of his accidents decreased, Petty was able to compete with any car on the track. As Lee Petty drove car number 42, Richard chose the number 43 for his own car, in tribute to his father and boss.

Lee Petty gave Richard the choice of either racing for a percentage of his winnings, or receiving a modest regular salary. He chose the weekly paycheck, a wise decision given the trials of that first season, and the arrangement continued for several years.

Richard Petty's second season as a NASCAR competitor was 1959. The year began with the opening of the Daytona International Speedway and the first running of the Daytona 500. A new era of stock-car racing was about to begin.

William France, the founder of NASCAR, had built the enormous 2½-mile track as the ultimate speedway. Daytona offered an exciting new brand of racing, with steeply banked turns that enabled the cars to keep their high speeds as they went into the turns. It also had a "tri-oval" shape with four turns, including one right before the main grandstand and finish line. It was a big change from the half-mile flat dirt tracks that were used for stock-car racing.

Race cars had grown increasingly powerful in the first 10 years of NASCAR racing, and the top speeds now approached 160 miles per hour. Daytona's size and shape allowed the cars to

The number 73 Thunderbird driven by Johnny Beauchamp was at first thought to have won the first Daytona 500. But photographs showed Lee Petty, in the number 42 Plymouth, actually beat him, and Petty was awarded the trophy. Joe Weatherly, in the Chevrolet at top, was a lap behind.

compete at higher speeds than ever before. France believed that this type of racing would attract even greater numbers of fans to stock-car racing.

He was correct. Daytona drew large crowds from the opening race, and the Daytona 500 soon became the biggest event of the NASCAR season. Despite the tremendous cost of building it, Daytona International Speedway became a big success.

Richard Petty was among the NASCAR drivers who arrived at Daytona for the first race in February. While practicing on the big new track, Petty made an interesting discovery. When two cars were running one behind the other with only a few feet between them, the first car created a vacuum, or "draft," that pulled the second car with it. The driver of the second car could lift his foot from the gas pedal and save fuel (and wear on the engine) without losing speed. There was also a benefit for the first car, which received a forward "push" from the air that was being moved forward by the second car.

This "drafting" technique also worked with a long line of race cars. While other drivers had occasionally encountered and used this phenomenon at smaller tracks in the past, Petty was apparently the first to experience the effect at Daytona. Nowadays, drafting is a common strategy at superspeedway races; at Daytona's high speeds, it is essential for success and not a mere curiosity.

Despite his useful discovery, Petty had a disappointing race at the first Daytona 500. Driving a convertible, Richard had engine trouble and had to retire after just eight laps.

Lee Petty had a better day. He won the race in a finish that was so close that the result was only determined four days after the race by studying a photo taken at the finish line.

Richard Petty's 1959 season was more successful than his first year. Accidents were rarer and his performances were far more consistent. At a race in Atlanta, Georgia, it appeared that Petty had captured his first victory, until the second-place driver protested that one of his laps had not been counted. It turned out he was correct, and Petty was placed second. The driver who had lodged the successful protest was none other than Lee Petty! The elder Petty went on to win his second consecutive driving championship in 1959, his third title in NASCAR's 11 years of racing.

Shortly after he had begun racing, Richard Petty returned to his old school, Randleman High, to attend a game. While he was there, he noticed a pretty cheerleader. After the contest, he introduced himself. Lynda Owens, who was five years younger than Petty, remembered first noting Petty's "pretty brown eyes." They began dating and soon fell in love.

In 1959, they quietly drove to South Carolina and got married. Richard was 22 years old and Lynda was just 17. Knowing that their families would not approve, they did not tell anyone. Each continued to live with their parents. Lynda returned to high school for her senior year and was Randleman High's homecoming queen.

When the news of their wedding became known, both sets of parents were displeased but took no action to break up the marriage. The young couple finally moved in together. The first child, a boy named Kyle, was born in June 1960,

In 1961, Lee Petty's car went over the wall at Daytona. He survived, but his racing career did not last much longer.

and three daughters, Sharon, Lisa, and Rebecca, soon followed.

Nineteen-sixty was a breakthrough season for Richard Petty. He no longer drove a convertible; and it marked the first season that he raced the entire schedule of Grand National events. Petty captured third place at the Daytona 500, narrowly edging his father, who finished fourth. Several weeks later, he finally won a race, a 100-miler in Charlotte. The first-prize money was $800. He won two more times during 1960, and ran consistently all season. Petty finished the season in second place in the drivers' standings, an impressive performance. Lee Petty finished sixth.

The 1961 season started poorly for both Pettys. During the first of two qualifying races held to determine the starting positions for the Daytona 500, Richard collided with another driver and his Plymouth went sailing over the outer wall and out of the track. Somehow, he escaped serious injury.

In the second qualifier, however, Lee Petty was involved in a similar incident with Johnny Beauchamp. Both cars were knocked over the rail. And this time, both drivers were seriously injured. Beauchamp was forced to retire from racing and Lee Petty suffered a badly injured leg that required several operations. He returned to racing, but without the same enthusiasm for the sport. Already past the age of 50, then an advanced age for a racer, Lee Petty competed only a few more times before retiring in 1964. When he left, he not only stopped driving but also turned over much of the responsibility for the management of Petty Enterprises to Richard.

Following his and his father's crashes at Daytona, Richard Petty's 1961 season was disappointing. He won only two races and finished well down in the standings. Petty rebounded nicely in 1962, with an impressive total of nine victories that enabled him to finish second in the driver's rankings, between champion Joe Weatherley and third-place driver Ned Jarrett.

Richard Petty had another solid season in 1963, winning 14 races and again finished second in championship points to Joe Weatherly. Most of his wins, though, came at smaller tracks. He had now been racing for six years, and while he had earned the respect of his fellow drivers and the appreciation of numerous fans, he had yet to make his mark.

At this point, if asked who the greatest driver in America was, few people would have thought to answer Richard Petty.

4

THE BEST EVER

As the 1964 season began, NASCAR was entering its 16th year of competition. The sport of stock-car racing was still growing and changing. Speeds were still increasing, with top marks now surpassing 170 miles per hour. Automobile manufacturers that had once ignored stock-car racing now started to sponsor teams, supplying much-needed technical and financial support to car owners and drivers. Stock-car racing's popularity continued to increase, and fans filled the tracks throughout the long racing season.

Even as its popularity spread, many of the sport's earliest stars were disappearing from the scene. Some, like Lee Petty and Buck Baker, had retired. Other drivers, like fan favorites Fireball Roberts and Joe Weatherly, were killed in racing accidents, and many other drivers suffered serious injuries that ended their racing careers.

Richard Petty mops his neck with a handkerchief after winning the Dixie 400 in 1966.

Developments in driver safety occurred slowly in stock-car racing's early years. Cars regularly went over the outer wall. As racing speeds increased, so did the number of serious injuries. This forced NASCAR and its drivers to focus their attention on improving driver safety. The goal was to build cars that would protect their drivers in an accident. Accidents could never be entirely eliminated, but perhaps a driver could escape without serious injury, even if his car was totaled.

Attention was also given to improving the handling and stability of the car, so that it would be less likely to skid or become airborne and leave the track. Fires were another frequent occurrence until new types of fuel tanks were developed that prevented or curtailed the spread of the flames.

Improved shoulder harnesses, seats, and roofs reinforced by "roll cages" were also introduced—and also saved many lives. As a result of these and other safety developments, drivers had a much better chance of surviving a serious crash or even walking away uninjured from a collision that would have been fatal a few years earlier.

Many of the safety advancements NASCAR helped develop at the beginning of the 1960s would later be used in normal passenger cars, saving thousands of lives every year. Petty Enterprises introduced several safety improvements that later found their way into many street cars.

By 1964, new stars were emerging to replace those who had departed. Ned Jarrett, who later became a well-known television racing commentator, became one of the sport's brightest young stars. A talented young driver from South

Carolina named David Pearson also began to win regularly on the Grand National circuit. In the next few years, Bobby Allison and Cale Yarborough added their names to the list of NASCAR stars. None of these drivers, however, would match the success of Richard Petty.

Not yet 27 years old, Petty announced his arrival as stock-car racing's newest star by capturing the 1964 Daytona 500. His car was by far the fastest on the field, and he won the face by a margin of a full lap over the second-place car. It was Petty's first win at the superspeedway, and he set a race record with an average speed of 154.344 miles per hour.

Petty continued his domination throughout the 1964 season. He won seven more races, and, most importantly, his Plymouth ran consistently well in almost every race. As a result, he finished high in the standings even in those races he did not win, and he ran in an incredible 61 races. His consistent performances earned him his first driver's championship at the end of the season. His 40,252 points put him well in front of Ned Jarrett, who had 34,950, and David Pearson, who had 32,146.

Petty's still-improving skills as a driver were a big reason for his success. He was able to combine his youthful courage with his increasing driving knowledge and superior reflexes, and the result was a triumphant 1964 season for Petty and his baby-blue number 43.

Another reason for Petty's dominance was the engine in his car. Chrysler had introduced a powerful new hemispherical engine for its Plymouth and Dodge models. The "hemi," as it was called, was a new design that met NASCAR's engine-

Just seconds after this picture was taken, Petty's supercharged dragster veered off the track and into the crowd, killing an eight-year-old boy and injuring eight other spectators. Petty was greatly disturbed by the accident and gave up drag racing shortly afterwards.

size restrictions, yet produced far more power than other manufacturers' engines. Petty and the other Chrysler drivers were the only people to run the hemi engine in 1964. Although they did not win many races, it became evident that hemi cars consistently ran at faster speeds than their competitors.

Bill France and the NASCAR leadership grew concerned that a handful of cars had a strong advantage over their opponents. Citing the interests of fair play, competition, and safety, NASCAR banned the hemi engine from its races at the beginning of the 1965 season. Angered by a rule change that seemed aimed mostly at him, Richard Petty withdrew from NASCAR racing.

Petty returned to Petty Enterprises in Level Cross, North Carolina, and built a car for drag racing—head-to-head competitions against other drivers on a quarter-mile straightaway. He had some success on the drag-racing circuit, but his enthusiasm for his new career was badly damaged due to a tragic accident. At a race in Dallas, Georgia, Petty lost control of his car, which then plowed into the grandstand. A young boy in the crowd was killed. Petty was deeply shaken by the incident.

In the middle of the 1965 season, NASCAR changed its policy and allowed the return of the hemi engine. Petty ended his brief retirement and returned to Grand National racing for 14 races. He won five of them.

Petty Enterprises had become a formidable race team. Besides Richard's accomplishments on the racetrack, Maurice Petty had developed into one of the best engine builders in stock-car racing. Cousin Dale was an able crew chief, in charge of the pit crew and race arrangements. Although retired from racing, Lee Petty still made the major decisions for the family business. All four men loved stock-car racing and had remained fully committed to Richard's success.

In addition, Petty Enterprises often entered a second car in races, with a serious of capable drivers piloting the second vehicle. One of these racers, Pete Hamilton, won three races while driving for the Pettys.

After missing the 1965 race due to his short "retirement," Petty captured the 1966 Daytona 500 in a race that was shorted by rain to 495 miles. He set a new record with an average speed of over 160 miles per hour, smashing the mark he had established in his 1964 victory.

Petty won eight more races over the rest of the 1966 season, including another superspeedway victory at the Atlanta Motor Speedway in August. Still, he only finished third in the chase for the driving championship.

Not yet 30 years old, Petty had already won 49 NASCAR races. That placed him in the top five drivers in the career victories category. He had started to make his mark. But the best was yet to come.

In 1967, Richard Petty had the greatest season of his career.

Actually, he had the best year any driver could ever hope to have.

Petty leads Paul Goldsmith on his way to his second Daytona 500 victory in 1966.

That year, Petty won an astounding total of 27 races. That's a record that no one has challenged seriously since. He also took second in seven others. And he only entered in 48 contests! During one amazing streak, Petty won 10 straight races.

An often repeated joke in 1967 was that the only big news to come from racing was when Richard Petty *didn't* win a race. Almost 30 years later, only 15 drivers have won more than 27 races in their *career*.

All year long, it seemed that Petty could do no wrong. It was not simply a matter of having the fastest car on the track at every race. He drove with a skill unmatched by any other driver. Confident but not cocky, Petty had learned that sometimes the best move during a race is the one you do not make. Aggressiveness can help a driver, but it can also lead him to make the mistake that costs him the race. In 1967, Petty showed the world how race cars should be driven. By the end of the season, Richard Petty was a legend.

Petty did not triumph at Daytona that year. Still, it seemed that he won everywhere else on the Grand National schedule. He even notched two victories at Darlington, the South Carolina track where he had previously had little success. He captured the checkered flag in two 500-mile races, at Darlington and at Rockingham, North Carolina.

Petty started the season a popular driver. At the end, he emerged as a clear fan favorite. Many were attracted by his driving skills, but his personality also won him many admirers. The handsome young driver with the warm, sincere smile was always polite to fans. Throughout the rest of his career, Petty was as loyal to his fans as they were to him. After a race, he usually spent an hour or two chatting with his fans, and staying until the last autograph request was satisfied.

Petty was also popular with sportswriters, who usually found him to be cooperative and patient with their questions. It was the writers who gave him his nickname, "The King," as a result of his overwhelming performance in 1967.

Despite his success, Petty's life away from the racing world changed little. He and his growing family still lived in a modest home in Randleman. His race cars were still built, adjusted, and repaired in the Petty Enterprises garage next to Lee Petty's home. Many of Petty's closest friends were childhood pals, who found their old friend remarkably unchanged by his fame.

Petty's marriage to Lynda was a very happy one. He was a good father to his four children, despite the constant traveling necessary for his career that frequently kept him away from home during the racing season.

Despite his accomplishments on the racetrack, Petty remained modest and friendly, a genuinely nice man who did not believe that he was very different from the fans who cheered him on. It was Petty's philosophy to "treat people like you'd like to be treated." This admirable outlook only increased his tremendous popularity.

An intense competitor on the racetrack, Petty never lost control of his emotions during a race. He did not become involved in feuds with other drivers, as often occurred in racing, although his duels with David Pearson and Bobby Allison produced much exciting racing. His competition with the other drivers ended when the race was over; afterward he was friendly and helpful to his competitors. He was almost always willing to answer a question or offer advice to another driver. As a result, no driver was more respected by his fellow racers than Richard Petty.

Because of his popularity, there was very little resentment of his overwhelming success in 1967. Some suspected that Petty Enterprises was somehow breaking the rules to improve the performance of Petty's car, but no evidence of cheating was ever found by NASCAR inspectors.

Still, one person tried to see to it that someone besides Richard Petty won a race that year.

It was late in the season, after Petty had won nine races in a row. At North Wilkesboro, North Carolina, the right rear tire on car number 43 went flat around the 40th lap. Petty had to make an unscheduled pit stop to have it replaced. As he charged back into the race, now a significant distance behind the leader, his crew discovered an inch-long nail in the flat tire. They could tell from the placement of the nail that Petty hadn't just accidentally run over it. Someone, perhaps a frustrated crew member from a rival racing team, had deliberately inserted the nail into the tire before the race.

This criminal sabotage could have caused a serious accident for Petty, but fortunately the only damage was to his standing in the race. It took him 60 laps before he was able to grab the

Petty's intensity can be seen here as he gestures excitedly at his tires and shouts to his pit crew.

lead. And he finished the race with the second-place finisher a full two laps behind. It was Petty's 26th win of the season and the 75th of his career.

Petty's 10-race winning streak came to an end after his victory at North Wilkesboro, but he added one more win a month later at Montgomery, Alabama. Naturally, Petty won the driving championship for the 1967 season. His 6,028-point lead over the second-place finisher was the widest margin in NASCAR history.

No one could realistically expect Petty to equal his 1967 success the following season, and he did not. King Richard had a good but not spectacular year, winning 16 races, and finishing in third place in the driving championship. All but one victory, at Rockingham, came at short tracks.

The problem in 1968, Petty believed, was with the design of his car. He was unhappy with the current Plymouth models, as well as the support he received from the Chrysler Corporation. Chrysler did not respond adequately to his suggestions and requests to make the Plymouth cars more competitive.

Petty needed a car that would enable him to win, and if Chrysler would not offer such assistance, he would seek it elsewhere. He soon began discussions with Ford Motor Company, the other major support of stock-car racing and Chrysler's biggest rival.

By the beginning of the 1969 season, Richard Petty was driving a Ford Torino, ending a 20-year affiliation between Petty Enterprises and Plymouth. Many fans, who bought Plymouths mostly because Richard Petty drove them, briefly felt bereft by Petty's surprising move to Ford.

But they soon forgave their hero.

Other major changes, however, would soon occur for both stock-car racing and Richard Petty.

THE KING

$\mathbf{I}$n 1970 a deal was made with ABC Sports to televise nine races each year. This exposed stock-car racing to a large national audience for the first time.

A new superspeedway, built by NASCAR owners William France and his family, opened in Talladega, Alabama, that proved to be even faster than Daytona. Top speeds now approached 200 miles per hour, but due to safety improvements, there was a major reduction in the number of serious injuries and deaths related to accidents.

Despite all of this evidence of success, NASCAR was also facing some very serious problems. General Motors had withdrawn its support to drivers and their teams several years earlier and by 1970, Ford and Chrysler were also leaving stock-car racing. The financial support these manufacturers provided was important to

Cale Yarborough gave him a stiff challenge, but "King" Richard won his fifth Daytona 500 in 1974.

the sport, and without them it would be difficult for many teams to survive. The prize money alone was not enough to meet the expenses of the race teams.

Two important developments saved NASCAR. In December 1970, the organization signed a deal with R. J. Reynolds, a major tobacco company, to be the primary sponsor of Grand National racing. R. J. Reynolds, the manufacturer of Winston cigarettes, was looking for a way to advertise its products after the United States government banned cigarette ads from television and radio.

R. J. Reynolds offered a large cash award to the drivers who earned the most points in the race for the driver's championship, which was now called the Winston Cup. They also sponsored one of the races. The entire Grand National series—now shortened to 30 events—was renamed Winston Cup racing. Other big companies began to sponsor races, and as a result, there was a major increase in the amount of prize money.

The other development that rescued NASCAR occurred in 1972, and Richard Petty was the groundbreaker. Petty signed the first primary sponsorship deal with STP, a company that manufactured oil and gasoline additives. By adding STP's name and

Petty straps himself in before running in the 1972 Pennsylvania 500. That's a fire extinguisher beneath his helmet.

red logo to his famous number 43, Petty helped to advertise the products. Because of his success on the racetrack, Richard Petty was the best salesperson that STP ever had. He also appeared in television commercials for STP products. Between his racing successes and his television commercials, Petty became a familiar face even to those who did not follow stock-car racing.

In return for displaying the STP logo on his car, racing suit, and even sunglasses, Petty received significant funds from STP to run his team. As a result of STP's financial support, the money won on the racetrack was less critical to the ability of his team to pay its bills. Other drivers had received money from their sponsors in the past, but never the large sum that STP provided Petty.

After it became clear that Petty and STP both benefited from this arrangement, numerous other companies vied with each other to have leading drivers promote their products. Beer companies, food manufacturers, restaurant chains, auto-parts stores, department chains, and other large corporations began to make sure their names were prominently displayed wherever their drivers and cars appeared.

Eventually, this type of sponsorship became a necessity for a Winston Cup racing team to race competitively. Because of the expense of starting and maintaining a racing team, the era of drivers owning their own team virtually came to an end. By the 1980s and 1990s, only a few of the top drivers still owned their own teams. Many drivers made more money from product endorsements than from racing.

It was the beginning of an exciting new era for stock-car racing. The additional money and exposure for NASCAR allowed the sport to increase its popularity faster than ever before.

Driving a Ford for the first time, Petty completed a 1969 season that was only slightly more successful than the year before. His car ran more consistently but he won just nine races, seven fewer than in 1968. He finished second to David Pearson in the standings. Petty returned to Plymouth for a more successful 1970 campaign that produced 18 victories but only a fifth-place ranking in the drivers' championship.

Richard Petty (left) hit the wall and spun around at the 1973 Atlanta 500. Buddy Baker was able to keep going, but the collision knocked Petty out of the race.

Petty experienced the first serious crash of his career in 1970. The steering suddenly failed on his car, and he bounced off the outer wall and found himself headed back across the track and directly into a steel guardrail. The car hit the guardrail head on and at full force, and then started to tumble. Many observers doubted that Petty would survive the frightening accident.

Knocked cold by contact with the guardrail, Petty had to be removed from the destroyed automobile. He soon regained consciousness, and found that his only injury was a dislocated shoulder. He was back behind the wheel of his car several weeks later.

Petty had a spectacular 1971 season, the best performance since his great 1967 campaign. The King captured the Daytona 500 to begin the year, his third triumph in the big race and his first since 1966. An unusually close contest, the race had 48 lead changes.

Petty beat his fellow drivers to the checkered flag in a total of 21 races that year, including victories in 500-mile races at Atlanta, Dover (Delaware), and Rockingham, twice. Petty easily captured his third Grand National driving championship, tying him with his father for most wins.

Petty's fame was now such that he starred in a movie that was loosely based on his life story. Few critics called *43—The Petty Story* a wonderful film, but the King gave a likable performance.

Petty had another great year in 1972, the first season of Winston Cup racing and the first year of his sponsorship deal with STP. He won only eight races on the new shorter 30-race schedule, but the STP-Plymouth ran strongly all season. Fittingly, Petty won the first Winston Cup title and also his record-breaking fourth driving championship.

Petty started 1973 strongly, winning his fourth Daytona 500. But switching to Chrysler's other model, the Dodge, for the first time, he won only five more races that year. He finished fifth in the Winston Cup standings, his lowest finish since 1965, the year he was partly "retired."

The King rebounded from his disappointing year with two of the best seasons of his career. He won the 1974 Daytona 500, which should have been called the Daytona 450 as the race had been shortened by 50 miles due to a serious gasoline shortage then affecting the whole country. No other driver had won more than one Daytona 500, as Petty claimed his fifth win.

Petty also triumphed in superspeedway races at Rockingham, Talladega, Michigan International Speedway, and Pocono International Raceway. Aside from Daytona, Petty had long been known for his strength on the shorter tracks. In 1974, though, he ran extremely well on all of the larger tracks on the Winston Cup schedule, thanks to the strong engines that Maurice Petty built for his brother. Petty claimed another Winston Cup championship with the hard-charging Cale Yarborough a distant second.

Petty added 13 more victories in a repeat strong performance during the 1975 season. There was a thrilling last-minute win at the Firecracker 400, the July race held at Daytona. Petty took his fifth driving title, the second time he had been able to put back-to-back championships together.

As proof of his utter dominance, Petty had now won four championships in five years. And yet, Petty's competitors in these times included some of the greatest drivers in NASCAR history. Cale Yarborough, Buddy Baker, and Benny Parsons were all highly skilled and experienced drivers capable of capturing any race. Each of these drivers won more than 19 races in his career. Also, a talented young newcomer named Darrell Waltrip won his first two Winston races in 1975, the same year that 23-year-old Dale Earnhardt made his first appearance. Richard Petty's two leading rivals, however, were David Pearson and Bobby Allison.

Two years older than Petty, David Pearson had provided a constant challenge for Petty since 1963, his rookie season. Pearson was one of NASCAR's most successful drivers, winning 105 races during his career and capturing back-to-

back driving championships in 1968 and 1969.

Although Petty and Pearson banged fenders and "traded paint" in numerous races, the two had tremendous respect for one another. "The rivalry with David was bigger than any of the others," Petty commented. "It never got personal. It was all on the race track." He also called Pearson "the best driver I've driven against over a period of years." Their thrilling duel to the finish line at the 1976 Daytona 500, won by Pearson after Petty's rare mistake caused the two drivers to crash, was one of the most exciting moments in the history of NASCAR.

Although Bobby Allison was also a gifted and successful driver, his aggressive style on the track sometimes annoyed Petty and threatened to turn personal. On several occasions, Allison's tactics caused Petty to have an accident, and an

Richard Petty (left) checks his engine with his brother, Maurice, before a big race. Other members of Petty's crew were his father, cousin, and several other relations.

angry Maurice Petty once punched Allison after he had caused Richard to wreck.

Later, King Richard and Allison developed a mutual respect. "Richard and I would have a bitter race at one track," Allison later said, "but at the next race if there was anything I needed, I didn't mind asking if he would loan it to me. If he had it, he would give it to me, and I would do the same thing for him. But once the race began, we were back at it again."

After his tremendous seasons in 1974 and 1975, Richard Petty struggled to win over the next three years. He won just three times in 1976 and five times in 1977. Nineteen seventy-eight was the worst season he had experienced since he started in NASCAR. For the first time since 1959, Petty failed to reach Victory Lane even once.

Despite his lack of success, Petty remained the most popular driver in Winston Cup racing. Cheerful and polite with his fans and the press, Petty was a colorful and distinctive personality. He had grown a stylish mustache and, because his eyes were sensitive to bright light, he almost always wore dark glasses, which bore the STP logo. When not in his race car, he often sported a cowboy hat. He wore cowboy boots even when he was driving.

At this time, illness struck Petty. For several years he had suffered from a serious and painful stomach ulcer that caused him to lose a lot of weight. His handsome face grew thin and gaunt. As a result of the ulcer, he had a large portion of his stomach removed in an operation before the beginning of the 1979 season.

Still weak and in pain from the surgery only weeks earlier, Petty was behind the wheel of number 43 for the Daytona 500 and the start of the 1979 schedule. Frustrated with the performance of his Dodge, he switched to General Motors cars and brought an Oldsmobile to Daytona.

In an ending with an eerie similarity to his last-lap crash with Pearson in the 1976 race, leaders Donnie Allison (Bobby's younger brother) and Cale Yarborough were jockeying for the lead when they collided on the last lap. Because of the accident, both cars were knocked out of the race. Donnie and Bobby Allison got into a fistfight with Yarborough on the backstretch as the other cars streaked past them toward the finish line.

Richard Petty, who had been running in fourth place, half a lap behind the leaders, grabbed the lead. Darrell Waltrip pressed Petty hard, but Petty held on for the narrow victory. "I lucked into that one more than any race I ever won," Petty recalled.

Petty won only four more races the rest of the season, but he ran consistently all year. He finished most races high in the standings, thus earning valuable Winston Cup points under the circuit's complicated points system. The brash and outspoken Darrell Waltrip also had an excellent season. He was obviously one of Winston Cup's rising young stars, but he annoyed many of his fellow drivers by failing to show respect for Petty and other veterans.

Waltrip dominated the first half of the season, but Petty managed to overcome Waltrip's big lead in the point standings with his own consistent performances. In the closest contest in NASCAR history, Richard Petty's 4,830 points edged Waltrip's 4,819. At the age of 42, King Richard won his seventh driving title.

THE FINISH LINE

Richard Petty's successes on the racetrack became rare after his 1979 season. No longer a young man, he did not have the sharp reflexes, strength, and endurance to compete against drivers who were 15 or 20 years younger than him. Petty could still run well, and he captured several races each year through 1984. On these occasions where he would take the lead in a race, the crowd would erupt in cheers for their long-time hero. The fans' support for Petty remained strong, even as the victories became scarce.

Richard Petty suffered one of the most serious accidents of his racing career in 1980. While leading a race at Pennsylvania's Pocono International Speedway, a wheel broke on his car, sending it directly into the wall. He suffered a broken neck in the crash. Luckily, there was no

President Ronald Reagan invited Richard Petty, his wife, Lynda, and car number 43 to the White House after Petty won his 200th race.

damage to his nervous system and he escaped without any paralysis. Remarkably, he was back in his race car the following week, wearing a neck brace.

Petty received many lesser injuries during his long career. He once estimated that over the years he had broken two dozen bones in racing accidents, and he could not recall how many times he had broken ribs. Petty had a high tolerance for pain, and he ignored discomfort from his injuries that would have sidelined most drivers. Also as a result of his years behind the wheel, Petty lost much of his hearing to the loud roar of the engines.

Driving a Buick, Petty won his seventh and final Daytona 500 in 1981. Noticing relatively little tire wear on the Petty car in the closing laps, crew chief Dale Inman called for a "fuel only" pit stop, while the other leading cars were all replacing tires. Inman's brilliant strategy saved enough time to put King Richard in the lead after the pit stop, and he held off the charge of a faster Bobby Allison to win the race.

Dale Inman had been Petty's crew chief since the beginning of his career. Shortly after the win at Daytona, Inman resigned to join Dale Earnhardt's team. Petty and the rest of the team felt betrayed by Inman's sudden departure. The team morale suffered, and Petty struggled on the track for the rest of the season.

In the early 1980s, a new generation of drivers arrived in Winston Cup racing. Dale Earnhardt, nicknamed "Ironhead" early in his career because of his recklessly aggressive driving, was the most successful young racer. Darrell Waltrip, Bill Elliott, and Geoff Bodine were also among the best of the new breed. Another

Kyle Petty is the third generation of terrific Petty race-car drivers.

promising new talent was Kyle Petty, son of Richard and grandson of Lee.

Kyle joined Winston Cup racing in 1979, just before his 19th birthday, but did not win his first race until 1986. He shared his father and grandfather's love of racing, but it took Kyle several years to escape their enormous shadows. He drove for Petty Enterprises, where he also took on duties in the running of the business.

Unfortunately, Kyle found it difficult to work with his father, and the situation damaged the relationship between the two men. It was not until he joined another top quality racing team owned by businessman Felix Sabates that Kyle Petty emerged as a leading driver in the late 1980s and early 1990s.

In 1983, after Petty won a race at Charlotte Motor Speedway, the 198th victory of his career, a NASCAR inspector noticed that Petty's car, a Pontiac, had an engine that was larger than regulations allowed. Maurice Petty was responsible; he explained his actions by stating that he knew that other teams were also using oversized engines. He felt he had to do the same thing just to keep pace with the others. NASCAR allowed Petty to keep the victory, but took away the Winston Cup points and prize money he would have earned.

Richard and Maurice Petty left Petty Enterprises in 1984, allowing Kyle to take over the operation of the family business. It was a disaster for everyone. Kyle was unhappy with his new responsibilities, and Petty Enterprises lost so much money that Kyle closed the company down before the end of his first year.

Meanwhile, Richard Petty went to work as a hired driver for the first time in his career. Bankrolled by music executive Mike Curb, the new team got off to a good start. Petty won a race at Dover, Delaware, in May; he triumphed at the Firecracker 400 at Daytona on July 4. President Ronald Reagan was on hand to congratulate Petty on his 200th career win.

The Curb team struggled after the two victories, and went winless the rest of 1984. They also won no races in 1985. For the first time in 20 years, Richard was not in the top 10 of the Winston Cup point standings, although Kyle Petty made his first appearance that year.

Richard grew increasingly frustrated by the team's lack of success, and he hated being someone's employee. Before the 1986 season, Petty announced that he was reviving Petty Enterprises with his brother. Dale Inman, who had helped driver Terry Labonte capture the 1984 Winston Cup, also eagerly returned to assist his cousins. A rejuvenated Petty Enterprises returned to full activity.

Petty failed to win again in 1986 and 1987. Running far behind in the pack, he often found himself involved in accidents caused by the traffic congestion around him. There were whispers that Petty's driving skills had deteriorated and that his reflexes were no longer capable of avoiding collisions that occurred around him. It was also said that younger competitors tried to drive cautiously around Petty, avoiding the type of aggressive driving they might have used around their peers. No one, on the track or in the audience, wanted to see a living legend like Richard Petty involved in a serious accident.

At the 1988 Daytona 500, Richard Petty was involved in the most frightening accident of his career. At over 180 miles per hour, the back of his car began to skid. The flow of air got underneath his car and lifted it off the track. Number 43 began to roll. Seven times it turned over. It finally landed back on the track, but directly in the path of Brett Bodine's car. Bodine had no time to avoid Petty; at full speed his car struck the front of what remained of Petty's car.

When number 43 came to rest, the car was a smoking mass of twisted and tangled metal. Horror gripped the silent crowd. It was one of the worst crashes that anyone could remember. Was it possible that Richard Petty had survived?

Amazingly, not only was Petty alive, but he had somehow escaped serious injury. He suffered a fractured shoulder and a bruised ankle, but he was healthy enough that two days later he appeared on the television show "Late Night with David Letterman." Walking with only a slight limp, Petty received a standing ovation from the audience.

In 1989, Petty failed to qualify for a race for the first time in his career. At Richmond, Virginia, his slow time in the qualifying heats caused him to be only a spectator at the race. He found the experience "devastating," but there were several more races over the next few seasons where his slow qualifying times forced him to sit out the race.

Finally, near the end of the 1991 season, Richard Petty recognized that the time had come to retire. At a press conference, he announced the "Richard Petty Fan Appreciation Tour," a final good-bye season of racing.

Speedways were jammed with fans eager to see the King race on more time. At the Pepsi 400 (formerly the Firecracker 400) at Daytona in July, Petty's fast qualifying time placed him on the front row for the start of the race. He grabbed the lead briefly at the start of the race, and it was a thrill to see him racing at the front of the pack one more time.

The last race of Richard Petty's amazing career was at Atlanta Motor Speedway on November 15, 1992. During the race, Petty was involved in a minor collision that knocked off the oil cooler on his engine. As the oil leaked into the car's exhaust, it burst into flame. Suddenly it appeared that Petty's whole car was on fire, and horrified fans held their breath as the car headed onto the grass infield.

The fire looked far worse than it was, and Petty was not in serious danger. He drove the car toward a firetruck parked on the infield; the flames were soon extinguished. Later, Petty commented that it was "not the kind of blaze of glory I wanted to go out in."

Petty's crew took the car back to the garage and began to repair it. Although the car was badly damaged, the crew got it to run again. After the race ended, the 55-year-old Petty got behind the wheel one last time, and slowly drove his battered race car around the track one last time. The crowd stood and cheered, and many fans wept without embarrassment at the departure of the great Richard Petty.

Petty's career totals are astounding. He won 200 races, including seven Daytona 500s. He captured 55 superspeedway victories and 41 wins in 500-mile events. He started 1,180 races. In his 35-year career as a driver, he covered over 600,000 miles and made about 8,000 pit stops. No other driver comes close to these numbers. And Petty's seven driving-championships record was only tied by Dale Earnhardt in 1994.

Petty won $7,710,129 in prize money while behind the wheel. As a tribute to his many accomplishments, the car that Petty drove to his 200th victory is on permanent display at the Smithsonian Institution in Washington, D.C.

When Petty began racing, NASCAR and its drivers were still struggling to survive. Races were held in front of small but enthusiastic crowds, and the drivers competed as much for the thrills as for the small prize money. By the time Petty retired as a driver, stock-car racing had become one of the most popular sports in America, with every speedway packing the fans in, and every race telecast to millions more at home.

Now a car owner, Petty is still a familiar face at the races, although he admits to feeling "lost" on race days. He occasionally works as a television commentator for Winston Cup events.

Petty still lives in Level Cross, not far from his parents. A small museum now stands next to Petty Enterprises for the thousands of fans who come to visit each year.

In 1992, Petty waved to his legions of fans at his last Daytona 500.

No sports figure is as beloved by his fans as Richard Petty. They remain devoted to their hero even in his retirement. Most of Petty's accomplishments from his 35-year career as a driver will never be equaled. In the exciting world of stock-car racing, Richard Petty will always be the King.

STATISTICS

Top 5 DRIVING CHAMPIONSHIPS (WINSTON CUP)

1962		1968		1974		1980	
Joe Weatherly	30,836	David Pearson	3,499	**Richard Petty**	**5,037.750**	Dale Earnhardt	4,661
Richard Petty	**28,440**	Bobby Isaac	3,373	Cale Yarborough	4,470.300	Cale Yarborough	4,642
Ned Jarrett	25,336	**Richard Petty**	**3,123**	David Pearson	2,389.250	Benny Parsons	4,278
Jack Smith	22,870	Clyde Lynn	3,041	Bobby Allison	2,019.195	**Richard Petty**	**4,255**
Rex White	19,424	John Sears	3,017	Benny Parsons	1,591.500	Darrell Waltrip	4,239
1963		**1969**		**1975**		**1981**	
Joe Weatherly	33,398	David Pearson	4,170	**Richard Petty**	**4,783**	Darrell Waltrip	4,880
Richard Petty	**31,170**	**Richard Petty**	**3,813**	Dave Marcis	4,061	Bobby Allison	4,827
Fred Lorenzen	29,684	James Hylton	3,750	James Hylton	3,914	Harry Gant	4,210
Ned Jarrett	27,214	Neil Castles	3,530	Benny Parsons	3,820	Terry Labonte	4,052
Fireball Roberts	22,642	Elmo Langley	3,383	Richard Childress	3,818	Jody Ridley	4,002
1964		**1970**		**1976**		**1982**	
Richard Petty	**40,252**	Bobby Isaac	3,911	Cale Yarborough	4,644	Darrell Waltrip	4,489
Ned Jarrett	34,950	Bobby Allison	3,860	**Richard Petty**	**4,449**	Bobby Allison	4,417
David Pearson	32,146	James Hylton	3,788	Benny Parsons	4,304	Terry Labonte	4,211
Billy Wade	28,474	**Richard Petty**	**3,447**	Bobby Allison	4,097	Harry Gant	3,877
Jim Pardue	26,570	Neil Castles	3,156	Lennie Pond	3,930	**Richard Petty**	**3,814**
1965		**1971**		**1977**		**1983**	
Ned Jarrett	38,824	**Richard Petty**	**4,436**	Cale Yarborough	5,000	Bobby Allison	4,667
Dick Hutcherson	35,790	James Hylton	4,071	**Richard Petty**	**4,614**	Darrell Waltrip	4,620
Darel Dieringer	24,696	Cecil Gordon	3,677	Benny Parsons	4,570	Bill Elliott	4,279
G. C. Spencer	24,314	Bobby Allison	3,636	Darrell Waltrip	4,498	**Richard Petty**	**4,042**
Marvin Panch	22,798	Elmo Langley	3,356	Buddy Baker	3,961	Terry Labonte	4,004
1966		**1972**		**1978**			
David Pearson	35,638	**Richard Petty**	**8,701.40**	Cale Yarborough	4,841		
James Hylton	33,688	Bobby Allison	8,573.50	Bobby Allison	4,367		
Richard Petty	**22,952**	James Hylton	8,158.70	Darrell Waltrip	4,362		
Henley Gray	22,468	Cecil Gordon	7,326.05	Benny Parsons	4,350		
Paul Goldsmith	22,078	Benny Parsons	6,844.15	Dave Marcis	4,335		
1967		**1973**		**1979**			
Richard Petty	**42,472**	Benny Parsons	7,173.80	**Richard Petty**	**4,830**		
James Hylton	36,444	Cale Yarborough	7,106.65	Darrell Waltrip	4,819		
Dick Hutcherson	33,658	Cecil Gordon	7,046.80	Bobby Allison	4,633		
Bobby Allison	30,812	James Hylton	6,972.75	Cale Yarborough	4,604		
John Sears	29,078	**Richard Petty**	**6,877.95**	Benny Parsons	4,256		

RICHARD PETTY: A CHRONOLOGY

1937   Born July 2, in Level Cross, North Carolina

1949   Father, Lee Petty, joins NASCAR's first season of racing; 12-year-old Richard works as father's pit crew

1955   Graduates from Randleman High School

1958   Drives in first race at Columbia, South Carolina

1960   Wins first race, at Charlotte, North Carolina

1964   Captures first win at Daytona 500; wins first driving championship

1965   Retires for much of year over dispute with NASCAR

1966   Wins second Daytona 500

1967   Wins 27 races, including 10 in a row, in greatest single-season performance in NASCAR history; becomes NASCAR leader in career victories; wins second driving championship

1971   Wins third Daytona 500 and third driving championship

1972   Signs sponsorship deal with STP; wins Winston Cup in its inaugural season

1974   Captures fifth Daytona 500; wins Winston Cup, his fifth driving championship

1975   Wins sixth driving championship

1976   Loses Daytona 500 in spectacular last-lap crash

1979   Captures seventh and last driving championship

1981   Wins seventh and last Daytona 500

1984   Wins 200th and last career victory at Daytona on July 4

1988   Escapes serious injury in horrifying crash at Daytona

1992   Retires from driving at age 54

SUGGESTIONS FOR FURTHER READING

Gaillard, Frye, with Kyle Petty. *Kyle at 200 M.P.H.* New York: St. Martin's Press, 1993.

Girdler, Allan. *Stock Car Racers.* Osceola, WI: Motorbooks International, 1988.

Golenbock, Peter. *American Zoom.* New York: Macmillan, 1993.

Huff, Richard. *Behind the Wall.* Chicago: Bonus Books, 1992

The Official NASCAR Preview and Press Guide. Charlotte, NC: UMI Publications, 1995.

Thorny, Al. *Fastest Man Alive.* Atlanta: Peachtree, 1989.

Vehorn, Frank. *A Farewell to the King.* Charlotte, NC: Down Home Press, 1992.

ABOUT THE AUTHOR

RON FRANKL was born in New York City and is a graduate of Haverford College. He is the author of *Duke Ellington, Charlie Parker* and *Miles Davis* for Chelsea House's Black Americans of Achievement series, *Bruce Springsteen* for the Pop Culture series, *Wilt Chamberlain* for the Basketball Legends series, and *Terry Bradshaw* for the Football Legends series. Mr. Frankl has been a fan of Richard Petty and stock-car racing for many years.

INDEX